Escape from

A fantasy adventure by Richard Brown

Series Editor: Louis Fidge

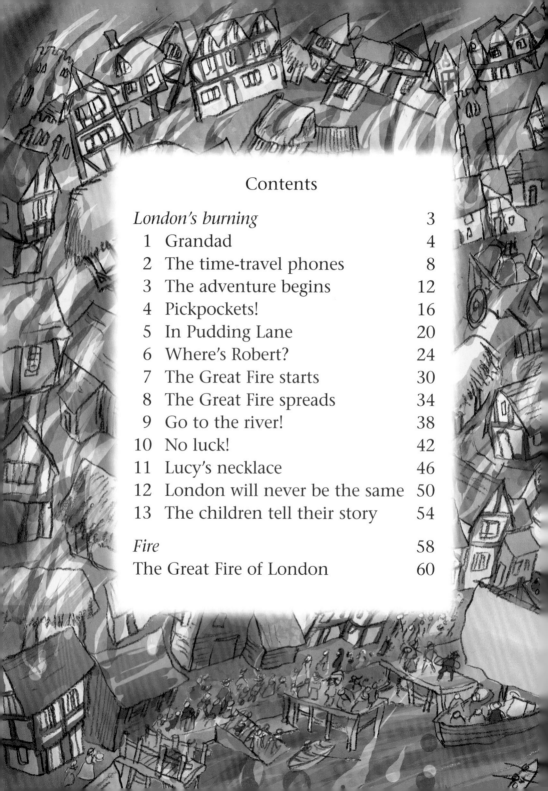

Contents

LONDON'S BURNING

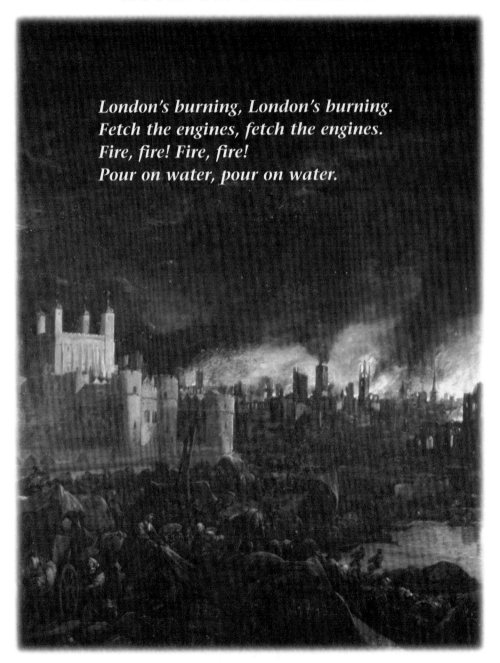

London's burning, London's burning.
Fetch the engines, fetch the engines.
Fire, fire! Fire, fire!
Pour on water, pour on water.

CHAPTER 1

Grandad

Robert was excited. He was going to stay with his grandfather at the weekend. Lucy, his cousin, was going to stay too. She was the same age as Robert and they were good friends.

Suddenly, the telephone rang. Robert answered it. It was Lucy.

'I hope we have a great weekend,' said Lucy.

'So do I,' said Robert. 'It's always good fun at Grandad's.'

There were two things about Grandad that Robert and Lucy really liked. First, he was very clever. He was an inventor. He invented lots of things, but mostly he invented new kinds of mobile phones.

The other thing they liked was that Grandad loved history. His house was full of history books. When Robert and Lucy came to stay, Grandad told them exciting stories from history. The cousins loved the stories because they were true.

Robert knocked on Grandad's door. Mrs Green, the maid, opened it.

'Hello, Robert,' she said. 'Come in.'

'Hello, Mrs Green,' Robert said. 'How are you?'

'I'm fine,' said Mrs Green. She took his bag from him. 'Your grandfather is in his study.'

Robert hurried into Grandad's study. 'Hello, Grandad,' he began. Then he stopped in surprise.

Grandad was sitting in an armchair. His foot was bandaged.

'Grandad, what happened?' Robert asked.

'I've hurt my ankle,' Grandad said. 'The doctor says I mustn't walk on it for a few days.'

'Poor Grandad. Does it hurt? I'll help you, and so will Lucy. Where is she? Has she arrived yet?'

Grandad looked worried. 'I'm not sure,' he said. 'I think she has disappeared.'

'Disappeared?' said Robert. 'What do you mean?'

Grandad leaned towards him and whispered, 'I think she has travelled back in time.'

CHAPTER 2
The time-travel phones

Robert looked at Grandad, amazed. 'How could Lucy have travelled back in time?' he asked.

Grandad showed him a mobile phone. 'Look at this,' he said. 'This is not an ordinary phone. This is my newest invention.'

Robert thought the mobile phone looked ordinary. 'What's special about it?' he asked.

'Do you promise not to tell anyone?'

'Not even Lucy?'

'Lucy knows already.'

'Not even Mum and Dad?'

'I'll tell them soon.'

'Okay. So what does it do?' asked Robert.

'With this mobile phone you can travel back in time.'

'Wow!' Robert exclaimed. 'Can you really do that?'

Grandad nodded proudly. 'I've worked on this invention for two years,' he said. 'It's ready now.'

Robert's eyes widened. 'How does it work?'

'Let me show you. You put in the date you want to visit. Then you put in the place you want to visit. Then you put in the password, *Adventure*.'

'Did you tell Lucy this?'

'Yes. And now one of the time-travel phones is missing.'

'How many time-travel phones have you made?' Robert asked.

'Four.' Grandad shook his head. 'I'm worried, Robert. I think Lucy has used the missing phone to travel back in time.'

'Wow!' Robert exclaimed. 'Where do you think she has gone?'

Grandad picked up a book. 'We were looking at this together last night,' he said. 'It's about the Great Fire of London in 1666.'

'I think I've heard about that,' said Robert. 'What happened?'

'In the early morning of 2nd September 1666, a baker's shop caught fire. The shop was in Pudding Lane, in London. There was a strong wind that night and the fire spread quickly. The fire grew so strong that no one could put it out. It burned for five days. It destroyed three-quarters of London. It was a huge disaster.'

Robert looked scared. 'Do you think that's where Lucy has gone?'

'Yes,' said Grandad. 'She was really interested in the story of the Great Fire.'

'But why can't she come back home?'

'To come home you have to spell the password backwards, then put in the place, then the date. I didn't tell her about that.'

'What shall we do?' said Robert.

Grandad pointed to his ankle. 'I can't walk,' he said, 'so I can't go and find her.'

'Then I'll go,' said Robert. He jumped up from his chair. 'I'll bring Lucy home.'

'You are a brave and clever boy,' said Grandad. 'I'm sure you can do it. But you must be very careful. Find Lucy and bring her home straight away. Don't wait until the fire starts.'

'Where shall I start?'

'Go to Pudding Lane. I'm sure that's where she will go first.'

CHAPTER 3

The adventure begins

Robert took the time-travel phone and put in the date and place: 1st September 1666, London. Then the password: *Adventure*. He pressed the green button.

Everything went dark. There was a sound like the wind rushing.

Then Robert was no longer in Grandad's study. He was standing in Thames Street, London, in 1666. The houses looked very different. The people wore different clothes.

On the right was a dark lane going to the River Thames. Robert could see a bridge with houses and shops on it. Crowds of people were walking over it. Other people were in carts or on horses. On the left was another lane, where tall houses leaned close to one another. The lane was too narrow for carts.

The air was hot and dusty. The street was full of dirt and rubbish. Clouds of dust rose from the wheels of the carts and there was a strong smell in the air.

Suddenly, a cart came towards Robert. It was going very fast. Robert jumped out of its way just in time. He bumped into a man who was selling water. The man was angry and shouted at him.

Then Robert heard a woman call, 'Hey, you, boy!'

Robert turned and saw a rich lady wearing a beautiful dress. She leaned out of the window of her chair and looked at Robert. She held a bag of sweet-smelling herbs.

'What extraordinary clothes you are wearing,' the lady said. 'Come closer. Let me look at you.'

Robert wore jeans, a T-shirt and trainers. Other people stopped and looked at him, too. He didn't like this. He had to find Lucy and bring her home quickly.

'Excuse me,' he said to the rich lady. 'Could you tell me where Pudding Lane is?'

She did not answer straight away. She said, 'How strange you look. You are so clean. It's most extraordinary! Where do you come from, boy?'

'I come from London.'

'And why are you wearing those strange clothes?'

'I'm looking for my cousin Lucy. Can you tell me where Pudding Lane is?'

'It's just over there,' said the lady. She pointed with her fan.

'Thank you,' said Robert. He ran quickly to escape from all the people who were staring at him. He ran down Thames Street and into Pudding Lane. It was dark and narrow.

He could not see Lucy anywhere. He shouted her name. He walked up the lane and stopped outside a baker's shop.

'This must be where the Great Fire began,' Robert said to himself.

A man came out of the shop. He was carrying a basket of loaves. He called to his daughter in the shop, 'I won't be long, Hannah.'

Robert watched the baker walk down the lane.

CHAPTER 4

Pickpockets!

Suddenly, two boys appeared out of an alley. They were dirty, ragged and had bare feet. They were a little older than Robert. They stared at his clothes. They pointed and laughed at him. Robert was scared and he tried to run away from them, but one of them grabbed him.

'Help!' Robert shouted.

'Doesn't he look strange,' said one of the boys.

'Leave me alone,' Robert said.

'Doesn't he speak strangely!' said the other boy.

The first boy pushed Robert. The other boy moved round behind him. His fingers reached towards Robert's pocket. Robert tried to get away, but the pickpockets were too strong for him.

'Hey!' came a loud voice above them. 'Leave him alone.'

The pickpockets saw another boy leaning out of a window above them.

'It's Toby!' one of the pickpockets said. 'Let's go!'

When Toby reached the street, the pickpockets had gone.

Robert got up. Toby was tall and strong. Robert realised why the other boys were scared of him.

'Thank you for your help,' he said. 'I think they wanted to rob me.'

'My name is Toby,' the boy said. 'Who are you?'

'I'm Robert.'

'Well, Robert, if you wear those clothes, people will think
you are strange. Why do you dress like that?'

'I come from the future,' said Robert. He grinned when
Toby looked surprised. 'I come from the twenty-first
century. But I'm sure you don't believe me.'

Toby came closer. 'I think I do,' he said. 'My sister, Molly,
met a girl with clothes like yours. She said the same thing.

She told us about the future.'

'Really?' said Robert excitedly. 'Is her name Lucy?'

'Yes. Do you know her?'

Robert nodded. 'She's my cousin. Our Grandad sent me here to take her home.'

'Lucy didn't say how she got here.'

'That's easy,' said Robert. 'Our grandfather's invented a time-travel phone. Let me show you.'

Robert put his hand in his pocket to get the phone – but it wasn't there!

'Oh, no!' he exclaimed. 'It's gone!'

'What has?'

'My time-travel phone.'

'I don't know what that is,' said Toby. 'But I think those boys have stolen it.'

CHAPTER 5

In Pudding Lane

'Without my time-travel phone, I can't go home,' Robert said.

Toby saw that Robert was very worried. 'Those boys could be anywhere by now,' he said.

'What shall I do?' asked Robert.

'Did Lucy use a time-travel phone to come here?' Toby asked.

'Yes!' said Robert. 'She's got a time-travel phone. She can go home and get another one for me. Thank you, Toby!'

Toby grinned. 'Come on. Lucy's at home with Molly. Let's go and find her.'

Toby lived in a tall, narrow house at the north end of Pudding Lane. As they went into the house, Toby whispered, 'We must be very quiet. My mother's in bed. She's not well.'

The boys climbed the dark stairs. In a small room, they found the girls. Lucy jumped up. She was very pleased to see her cousin.

'Robert,' she said. 'I've been so frightened. I tried and tried to go home but the time-travel phone does not work.'

Robert explained that she had to spell the password backwards. Lucy was pleased to hear that!

Toby looked at the time-travel phone. 'This looks amazing. I wish my father could see this,' he said.

'We can show it to him,' said Lucy.

'No, he's not here. He's a sailor and he's at sea now, far away.'

Robert said to Lucy, 'Some pickpockets stole my phone. Will you go home and get another one for me?'

Lucy put the password, place and date into her time-travel phone. She remembered to spell the password backwards. One minute she was there. The next minute she was not! Toby and Molly looked at each other in amazement.

'She'll be back soon,' said Robert, with a laugh.

Toby nodded. 'Hey,' he said. 'Would you like to explore London while you are here?'

'Yes, please,' said Robert.

Robert, Toby and Molly left the house and walked down Pudding Lane.

Robert stopped outside the baker's shop. 'Shall I tell the baker that the fire will start tonight? Maybe I can stop the Great Fire of London,' he thought.

'I'm going into the baker's,' he said to Toby and Molly. 'I won't be long.'

He went into the shop. 'Excuse me,' he said to Hannah, the baker's daughter.

She was putting some biscuits into a basket. 'Oh!' she exclaimed, looking surprised. 'What strange clothes you're wearing.'

'That's because I come from the future.'

She looked even more surprised. 'You come from the future?'

'Yes. I've come to tell you that a big fire will start here tonight and it will spread all over London.'

'Don't be silly!' Hannah said.

'But it's true. It will happen.'

'No one can see the future,' said Hannah. 'Please go, at once. Your friends are waiting for you outside.'

'But you *must* listen to me,' said Robert. 'Please.'

Then a man's voice behind him said, 'What is happening here?'

Robert turned. It was Thomas Farynor, the baker.

'Please sir, you must believe me. A big fire will start here tonight. I know it will.'

Mr Farynor did not look pleased. 'Don't be silly! Now please leave my shop.' The baker opened the shop door to let Robert out.

'But you must listen to me,' said Robert. 'Your shop will burn down tonight. Please believe me.'

The baker pushed him into the street.

CHAPTER 6

Where's Robert?

As the children walked into Thames Street, a gang of pickpockets jumped on them. Molly ran away, screaming. Toby tried to fight them but he was chased away.

The pickpockets caught Robert. They took him to a house in Fish Street Hill.

'Let me go!' Robert shouted.

The gang leader said, 'Give us another one of those things and we'll let you go.'

'But I haven't got another phone,' said Robert.

'Then we won't let you go,' the leader said.

'Why do you want a phone?' Robert asked.

The boys laughed. 'We sold the first one to a rich gentleman,' said the leader. 'He wants another one.'

'I haven't got another one,' said Robert.

The gang leader looked angry. The pickpockets locked Robert in a dark room at the bottom of the house.

'We'll come back tomorrow night. Give us another phone and we'll let you go,' the gang leader said.

It was hot and smelly in that room. Robert heard rats. He hated rats.

Moonlight came through a high window.

'Let me out!' Robert shouted, but no one came.

Robert grew more and more frightened. No one knew where he was. Then he remembered about the fire. He knew he must get out of that dark, smelly room.

Meanwhile, Lucy travelled back to the present. Grandad didn't want her to go back to 1666 again, but she had to help Robert.

Lucy returned to London in the afternoon. This time she had two time-travel phones with her.

When she arrived, Molly was washing Toby's cuts and bruises.

'Where's Robert?' Lucy exclaimed.

When they told her, she knew Robert was in real danger. 'We have to find him tonight,' she said. 'Before the Great Fire begins.'

'You still believe there's going to be a Great Fire tonight?' Molly said.

'Yes,' said Lucy. 'Now let's go and look for Robert.'

It was warm in the street and a strong, dry wind was blowing. They searched for Robert all that day. Toby talked to many people but no one knew where Robert was.

When night came, the children were still looking for Robert. At one o'clock they arrived at Fish Street Hill. They knocked on all the doors but no one answered. It was late and everyone was asleep.

Robert was still in the dark downstairs room. He awoke suddenly. Rats were running all over him. One bit his ankle. He screamed.

Outside, the children heard his scream.

'It's Robert!' Lucy exclaimed.

'Where?' Toby said.

'The scream came from that window,' Molly said.

She pointed to a small, dirty window. Robert was still shouting.

'Robert?' called Toby into the dark room.

'I'm here,' Robert answered.

Toby leaned in the window and reached down. 'Hold my hand,' he said, 'and I'll pull you up.'

The girls held on to Toby.

Robert climbed out of the window. 'Thank you,' he said. 'Oh, thank you!' Then he saw Lucy. 'You're back!' he exclaimed.

'Of course I am!' She laughed.

'Have you got another time-travel phone?'

Lucy took one from her pocket and showed it to him. '

CHAPTER 7

The Great Fire starts

Toby said. 'Hey, what's that smell?'

'It smells like something burning,' said Molly.

'Burning?' Robert exclaimed.

'It's the Great Fire!' said Lucy.

'Where?' Toby asked.

'In Pudding Lane. In the baker's. We told you.'

'But how do you know?' Toby said.

'It's in all the history books,' said Lucy.

Molly looked scared. 'Mother's not well. We must get her out of the house. Come on.'

They ran back through the moonlit streets and into Pudding Lane. The air smelled of burning and the wind blew smoke towards them. They began to cough.

'Look!' Toby shouted.

He pointed to the upstairs window of the baker's house. The window broke and glass fell down. Flames came out of the window.

'Who's inside?' Lucy asked, coughing.

'There's Mr Farynor,' said Toby, 'his daughter Hannah, and his servants. I hope they're all right.'

'Let's get Mother,' said Molly.

They ran past the baker's and into Toby's house. They woke his mother. The girls helped her downstairs, and onto the family's cart. Robert and Toby brought some of the family's things down.

The baker's house was now burning fiercely.

'Look!' Toby shouted. He pointed to the roof. They saw Thomas Farynor, Hannah and one of the servants, climbing along the roof towards their neighbour's house. 'They're going to escape,' Toby shouted.

'Where's Rose?' Molly said. But there was no sign of the other servant.

Thomas Farynor appeared in front of his burning building. He looked very upset. 'My gold,' he shouted. 'My gold's in there.'

The street filled with people. Some shouted to their neighbours. Others screamed in fear.

'We must get away from here,' Toby shouted.

'Take me to the hostel,' said his mother. 'We will be safer there.'

Now bells were ringing loudly to warn everyone that there was a fire.

The children and Toby's mother soon reached the hostel, and Toby's mother went to her room to rest.

Toby said, 'I wonder what's going on. I'm going out to see. Is anyone else coming?'

'I'll stay and look after Mother,' said Molly.

'I'll come,' said Robert.

'Let's go home,' Lucy said to her brother. 'Home to Grandad.'

'No,' Robert said excitedly. 'This is real history! Let's stay and see a bit of it, Lucy. Then we can go home.'

CHAPTER 8

The Great Fire spreads

The three children ran past the hostel's stables. The horses in the stables felt the danger. They were frightened and were neighing loudly and kicking at the doors.

In the street, the wind howled. Carts filled Thames Street. People were going towards a large building with thick stone walls.

In Pudding Lane, flames came through the roof of the baker's house. People passed buckets and bowls of water to some men who were pumping a fire engine. The children ran into Toby's house to get more bowls and buckets. But the fire engine was not powerful enough and the flames grew higher.

Later, the children stood in Thames Street and looked down Pudding Lane.

'Our house is not on fire yet,' said Toby. His face was black with smoke.

'It will be soon,' said Lucy, shaking her head.

'Please don't say that,' said Toby.

'I'm sorry. Soon everything from here to the Tower of London will be burned down.'

'What?' Toby exclaimed. He could not believe it.

Lucy nodded. 'I've read all about it in Grandad's history book. London is on fire.'

Just then a coach stopped nearby and a gentleman got out. He walked a little way into Pudding Lane and stood there with his hands on his hips.

'Who's that?' Robert asked.

'I think he's in charge of the soldiers,' said Toby.

But the gentleman shrugged his shoulders and said that there was nothing to worry about. It was only a small fire, he said. His soldiers weren't needed. He got back into his coach and drove away.

The lane was now full of people, carts and animals. They were all trying to escape.

'Look!' Robert exclaimed. He pointed up the lane. 'The house next to the baker's is catching fire now.'

For an hour the children watched as the flames spread from one house to another. The heat got stronger and stronger. Suddenly, there was a loud explosion. It knocked the children over. Luckily, no one was hurt.

'Let's go back to the hostel,' said Robert.

'That won't be safe for long,' said Lucy. 'The flames will soon reach it. We must take your mother to a safer place, Toby.'

CHAPTER 9

Go to the river!

They ran back to the hostel. Just as they arrived, the horses kicked down the stable doors and galloped into the streets. The children jumped out of their way just in time.

'Look,' said Robert, pointing to the sky. The wind blew hot ash and bits of burning wood into the air. These landed on roofs and set them on fire. Hot ash fell onto the hay near the stables. Soon the stables were on fire too.

Now there was noise everywhere. The wind howled and bells rang.

The children ran into the hostel and woke Toby's mother. They helped her onto the cart.

'We must go to the river,' she said. 'It'll be safer there. But first, I want to take a last look at our house.'

The children pushed the cart. It took a long time to reach Pudding Lane because everyone else was going in the other direction. When they arrived, they saw that the whole lane was now on fire. The thick smoke made them cough. They turned and headed for the river.

Toby's mother tried to get off the cart but she was too weak to walk.

The wind blew smoke, ash and burning hay and wood all about them.

Carts full of furniture and people headed along the streets to the river. People pushed, shoved and argued. They were frightened.

They reached Thames Street. But the road to the bridge was blocked.

'We must go to the river another way,' said Lucy. 'Soon the bridge will be on fire.'

'We can go down one of the alleys,' said Toby.

They pushed the cart along Thames Street away from the fire. The alleys were narrow and full of people trying to find another way to the river. At last they reached Black Raven Alley.

'I can see the river,' said Toby. 'Let's go down here and look for a boat. Our uncle Oliver lives near the river. We can row there and stay with him. Come on.'

They pushed the cart down the dark, smelly alley.

At the river bank, they stopped. People were walking through thick mud to reach the water. The river was full of boats carrying people and their things. Furniture floated on the water, and some of it was on fire.

'The river's very smelly,' said Lucy. She held her nose with her fingers.

'There's no time to worry about that!' said Toby. 'Let's see if we can find a boat.'

The boys left the girls to look after Toby's mother. They ran up and down the muddy river bank to try and find an empty boat. But all the boats were full.

CHAPTER 10

No luck!

'Look at the moon,' said Toby.

The moon was red. A cloud of thick, black smoke passed in front of it.

The boys saw an empty boat and ran towards it. They soon discovered why it was empty. The man wanted a lot of money for his boat.

Toby's mother did not want to pay. 'Toby,' she said. 'Go to Uncle Oliver's house. Ask him to bring his boat down river to pick us up.'

'But what if the fire reaches here before we get back?' Toby asked.

'Just go,' said his mother. 'Hurry, please.'

'I'm coming with you,' said Robert.

'You don't have to,' said Toby. 'You can go back to your own home now if you want. You will be much safer there.'

Robert turned to Lucy. 'He's right. We're in great danger here. Grandad will be worried. Shall we go home?'

Lucy shook her head. 'I'm staying here with Molly, to help her mum,' she said. 'But you go if you want.'

'I'll stay if you're staying. But if things get too dangerous, promise me that you will go. Don't wait for me.'

'I promise,' said Lucy.

By now it was dawn. As they looked back, the boys could see the glow of the fire above the roofs. They hurried away from the choking smoke and ash.

It was quieter in this part of the city. People looked out of their windows to see what was happening. They did not look worried. The fire will never spread this far, they thought.

'All their houses will be burned to the ground,' said Robert. 'I feel so sorry for them.'

No one looked at Robert's jeans and T-shirt any more. Now that his clothes were black with dirt and ash, they did not look any different to Toby's clothes.

For nearly an hour the boys hurried through the city. When they reached Uncle Oliver's house, they knocked on the door. No one answered. They knocked and knocked until a window opened upstairs and a servant girl appeared.

'The master and mistress have gone to your mother's house,' she said to Toby. 'They heard about the fire in Pudding Lane and they went there to help.'

'When they return,' Toby said to her, 'tell them that Molly, Mother and I are on the river bank near Black Raven Alley. Tell them that Mother's ill and Father's away. Tell them to bring a boat. And tell them to hurry. The fire is spreading quickly.'

'I will,' said the servant. 'Do you want to come inside?'

'No,' said Toby. 'We haven't time.'

'What shall we do now?' Robert asked.

'Let's see if we can find Uncle Oliver and Aunt Bess,' said Toby.

But the boys did not see them anywhere.

In Thames Street, every house and shop was on fire. It was too hot and too dangerous now. The boys ran from the fire as fast as they could.

CHAPTER 11

Lucy's necklace

Soldiers pulled down buildings with ropes and hooks. They tried to make a space to stop the fire spreading. But the strong wind blew wood and ash across the open space and onto the straw roofs of the houses on the other side. These roofs soon burst into flames and the fire spread. The wind was too strong.

The boys reached Black Raven Alley and ran down it. Molly and her mother were still there with the cart.

'Where's Lucy?' asked Robert.

'She's gone to find a boat,' said Molly.

'But the price for the boat will be too high now,' said her mother.

Toby told his mother that they did not find Uncle Oliver and Aunt Bess. She shook her head. 'What will happen to us now?' she said quietly.

'Look!' Robert exclaimed. He pointed to the bridge. The wooden houses on the bridge were on fire. People were jumping off the bridge into the water. The river was crowded with boats trying to escape from the burning bridge.

The houses in the alley started to catch fire. Flames soon spread towards the river bank.

Suddenly, Lucy appeared. 'Come quickly,' she said. 'I promised to pay the boatman my silver necklace to take us across the river. Hurry, or someone else will have the boat.'

The children pushed the cart towards the boat. People were trying to give the boatman money to use his boat, but he liked Lucy's necklace. He knew it was worth a lot of money.

The boatman helped Toby's mother to get into the boat. Then he helped them put their things in. There was just enough room left for the children. They all sat on the cart. At last they were ready to row across the river.

'Shall we go home?' Robert said to Lucy. 'They will be all right now, without us.'

'Let's wait until they are safely across the river, shall we?'

'That's what I wanted you to say!' Robert said with a grin.

The boatman began to row. The wind made the water rough. Molly felt sick and held onto her mother.

When they reached the middle of the river, they looked back at the burning city. Clouds of black smoke filled an orange-red sky. The children could still feel the heat of the flames.

All along the river bank there were crowds of people looking for boats to take them and their things to safety.

'It'll be much worse than this,' said Lucy. 'Soon, three-quarters of London will be on fire. This is only the start of it.'

CHAPTER 12

London will never be the same

Toby's mother shook her head in sadness. 'We have no home now,' she said.

'Where will you stay?' Robert asked.

'My sister, Nell, lives across the river with her family. We'll stay with her.'

'You'll be safe there,' said Lucy. 'The fire didn't spread south of the river.'

'But what about Uncle Oliver and Aunt Bess?' Molly said.

'They can come there too,' her mother replied. 'We'll be one big family then.'

The boat reached the other river bank.

In this part of the city, the streets were quieter. It was easier to push the cart. They arrived at Aunt Nell's house at ten o'clock.

When she opened the door, Aunt Nell looked at them in amazement. All their faces were black and they were covered in dust and ash. Aunt Nell did not recognise Toby, Molly or their mother!

Everybody washed, had a meal and felt better. Toby's mother went to bed and fell asleep at once. Toby and Molly told Aunt Nell about their adventures.

Then they became quiet. They were thinking of their home. They were tired after such a long and exciting night.

'We are lucky,' said Toby. 'We had somewhere to go. There must be lots of people with nowhere to go. They will have to sleep outside or go into the countryside.'

'This is only the first day of the Great Fire,' said Robert. 'It will burn for four more days. London will never be the same again.'

'Come on, Lucy' said Robert. 'It's time for us to go home now. Grandad will be worried about us.'

Robert turned to Toby. 'I'm sorry we came at such a sad time.'

'You helped us to escape. Thank you,' said Toby.

'I don't know if we will see you again,' Lucy said to Molly, 'but I will never forget you.'

'May I look at your time-travel phone again?' Toby asked Robert.

Robert gave him the phone. Toby pressed a few of the buttons. 'Perhaps one day I will travel to the future,' he said. He grinned, then handed the phone back.

'Thank you for giving your necklace to the boatman,' said Molly to Lucy.

Lucy smiled. She was sorry to lose her necklace but she was pleased to help.

'We must go,' said Robert.

The children waved goodbye. Robert and Lucy put in the password backwards and pressed the green buttons on their time-travel phones.

Everything went dark. There was the sound of wind rushing. Then they were back in Grandad's study.

CHAPTER 13

The children tell their story

Grandad smiled when he saw them. 'Welcome home!' he exclaimed.

The children both began to speak. Grandad held up his hand for silence. 'I can smell the fire and smoke in your clothes!'

'Can you?' said Lucy. She sniffed her T-shirt. 'Yes!' she said.

'So can I,' said Robert.

'That's what the Great Fire of London smells like,' said Grandad. 'Now go and change your clothes before you do anything else.'

They met Mrs Green, the maid, in the hall.

'What is that smell?' she asked.

'It's the Great Fire of London,' said Robert.

'Don't be silly,' said Mrs Green, with a laugh.

The children ran upstairs to change their clothes.

Later, they told Grandad the whole story.

'It's just like it says in the history books,' said Grandad. 'You were so lucky to see it. No one else in the world today has been there!'

'I never thought of that!' Robert exclaimed.

'But now you must give me the time-travel phones.'

'Do we have to?' Lucy wailed.

'I don't want you to travel in time by mistake. It's much too dangerous!'

They gave the phones to Grandad.

'One day,' he said, 'someone will find the missing phone. And people will say, "It is three hundred and fifty years old." They will be very surprised!'

'I hope we can go time-travelling again,' Lucy said.

'So do I,' said Robert. 'It's the most exciting thing I've ever done in my life.'

The new term began at school. Robert and Lucy were in the same class.

'This term,' said their new teacher, 'we are going to study some exciting events in history. I'm going to start with the Great Fire of London. Has anyone heard of that?'

Robert and Lucy grinned at each other and put up their hands.

The teacher folded his arms. 'Really? What do you two know about it?'

'Well,' Robert said, 'it began very early on 2nd September 1666, in a baker's shop in Pudding Lane, London.'

'It was a warm night,' said Lucy, 'and there was a strong wind. The wind helped to spread the fire.'

'Well done!' said the teacher. 'You know a lot about it.'

'We know a lot about the first day of the Great Fire,' said Lucy.

'Tell us more, then,' said the teacher.

So they did. Everyone in class was amazed.

'How do you know all this?' the teacher asked.

'Oh, we just like history,' said Lucy. 'Grandad tells us stories from history.'

'You make it sound as if you were there,' said the teacher, with a laugh.

'Perhaps we were,' said Robert, grinning.

'Perhaps we travelled back in time,' said Lucy.

The teacher smiled. 'I wish we could do that. History would be very easy to learn!'

'And it would be more fun,' said Robert.

All that term the cousins thought about the time-travel phones in Grandad's safe.

'One day,' said Lucy, 'perhaps we will go time-travelling again.'

'I hope so,' said Robert. 'Where will we go next, do you think?'

FIRE

Fire is alive, like you and me.
Fire can be a friend – or an enemy!

Fire can be a friend to girl or boy.
Fire can dance and leap with joy.
Fire can make us happy – all red and gold.
Fire can keep us warm when we're cold.
Fire can chase sadness from our lives.
Fire can melt metal for forks and knives.

Fire is alive, like you and me.
Fire can be a friend – or an enemy!

Fire can be an enemy, and burn our homes.
Fire can be a monster when it roams.
Fire eats everything in its path.
Fire crackles and cackles with an evil laugh.
Fire doesn't care what it destroys –
Trees, houses, babies' toys.

Fire is alive, like you and me.
Fire can be a friend – or an enemy!

Louis Fidge

THE GREAT FIRE OF LONDON

How did the Great Fire of London start?

It started in a baker's shop, in Pudding Lane. The baker, Thomas Farynor, his daughter Hannah and a servant escaped over the rooftop to a neighbour's house. Their maid, Rose, did not escape.

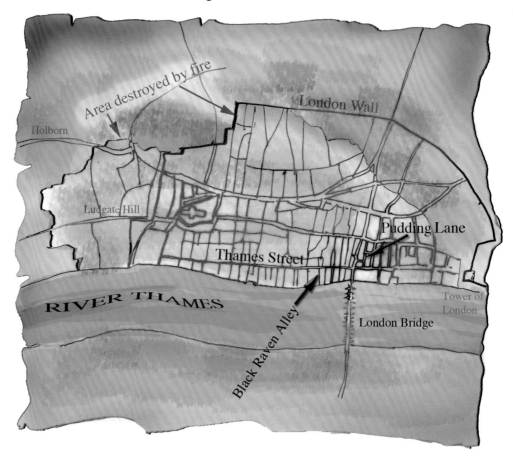

How long did the fire last?

The fire lasted for five days.

How much of London did the fire destroy?

It destroyed about three-quarters of the city. An area about 2.5 kilometres long and 60 metres wide was burned to the ground.

What did the fire destroy?

It destroyed over 13,000 houses and many other buildings. Lots of valuable books and manuscripts and other treasures were lost in the fire.

How many people died?

Most people believe that hundreds, perhaps thousands, of people died in the Great Fire.

Why did the fire spread so quickly?

- ten months without rain meant everything was very dry
- most buildings were made of wood, plaster or paper
- the buildings were very close to each other
- there was a strong wind
- the wind carried burning ash in the air, and the ash set fire to straw roofs
- the fire engines could not pump enough water onto the fire
- there wasn't enough water to put out the flames

Why didn't the fire spread across the River Thames to the south of the city?

The wide river stopped the fire from spreading to the other side. There was only one bridge, and the fire only burned half of it. Burning ash that blew across the river was put out before it caused a fire.

How did the fire end?

The king's brother told the soldiers to pull down buildings near the fire. This stopped it spreading further. Also, the strong wind stopped.

What happened to the people who lost their homes?

They moved to areas outside London. Some lived in tents. Most people built huts to live in. Slowly they built the City of London again. They used brick and stone instead of wood. The new buildings did not burn so easily.

How do we know about the Great Fire of London?

People wrote about it in diaries, letters and reports.

Macmillan Education
Between Towns Road, Oxford OX4 3PP
A division of Macmillan Publishers Limited
Companies and representatives throughout the world

ISBN 978-1-4050-6018-9

Design and layout by Anthony Godber
Illustrated by Mike Spoor
Cover design by Linda Reed & Associates
Cover illustration by Mike Spoor

The authors and publishers are grateful for permission
to reprint the following copyright material.
'Fire' © Louis Fidge 2006,
reprinted by permission of the author.

The authors and publishers would like to thank the following
for permission to reproduce their photographic material:
Getty Images/Hulton Archive p3

Printed and bound in Malaysia

2011 2010
10 9 8 7 6 5